LEARNING ABOUT THE EARTH

Lakes

by Emily K. Green

BLASTOFF! READERS 3

BELLWETHER MEDIA · MINNEAPOLIS, MN

Note to Librarians, Teachers, and Parents:

Blastoff! Readers are carefully developed by literacy experts and combine standards-based content with developmentally appropriate text.

Level 1 provides the most support through repetition of high-frequency words, light text, predictable sentence patterns, and strong visual support.

Level 2 offers early readers a bit more challenge through varied simple sentences, increased text load, and less repetition of high-frequency words.

Level 3 advances early-fluent readers toward fluency through increased text and concept load, less reliance on visuals, longer sentences, and more literary language.

Whichever book is right for your reader, Blastoff! Readers are the perfect books to build confidence and encourage a love of reading that will last a lifetime!

This edition first published in 2007 by Bellwether Media.

No part of this publication may be reproduced in whole or in part without written permission of the publisher. For information regarding permission, write to Bellwether Media Inc., Attention: Permissions Department, Post Office Box 1C, Minnetonka, MN 55345-9998.

Library of Congress Cataloging-in-Publication Data
Green, Emily K., 1966–
   Lakes / by Emily K. Green.
      p. cm. — (Blastoff! readers) (Learning about the Earth)
Summary: "Simple text and supportive images introduce beginning readers to the physical characteristics and geographic locations of lakes."
   Includes bibliographical references and index.
   ISBN-10: 1-60014-037-8 (hardcover : alk. paper)
   ISBN-13: 978-1-60014-037-2 (hardcover : alk. paper)
   1. Lakes—Juvenile literature. I. Title. II. Series.

GB1603.8.G74 2007
551.48'2–dc22   2006000565

Text copyright © 2007 by Bellwether Media.
Printed in the United States of America.

Table of Contents

A lake is a large pool of water surrounded by land.

Fresh water fills most lakes. Fresh water is not salty.

Glaciers made many lakes. Glaciers are big blocks of ice. Long ago, glaciers covered many parts of the earth.

Glaciers **carved** holes in the land as they moved. The melted ice filled the holes and became lakes.

Lakes come in many sizes. Some lakes are small. A small lake is sometimes called a pond.

Some lakes are big. Some lakes are even too big to see across.

The edge of the lake is called the shore. In some places, sand and rocks cover the shore.

In some places, plants grow along the shore.

Some lakes are **shallow**.

Sunlight can reach the bottom of shallow lakes. Plants can grow where there is sunlight.

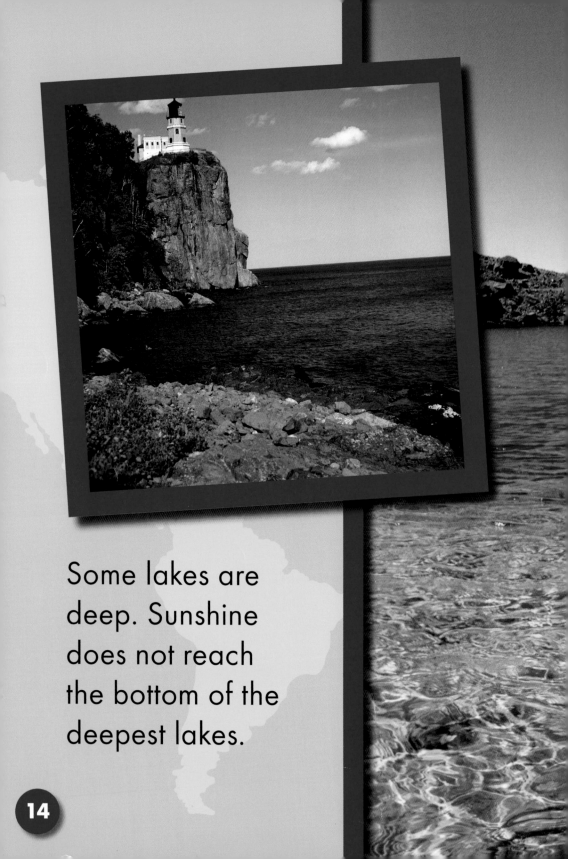

Some lakes are deep. Sunshine does not reach the bottom of the deepest lakes.

Most lakes are shallow
near the shore and
deeper in the middle.

Many types of fish live in lakes.

Fishing is a popular
sport at most lakes.

Lakes are filled with tiny plants
called **algae**. Algae turns
sunshine into **oxygen**. Plants
and fish living in the lake
need oxygen.

Sometimes there is too much algae in a lake. This can turn the water bright green.

In winter lakes may freeze. Only the top of the lake freezes. The water doesn't freeze all the way to the bottom. Fish live in the water under the ice.

In spring warm air and sunshine melt the ice. Soon the lake will have open water again.

Glossary

algae—tiny plants that live in lakes

carve—to cut through

glaciers—giant blocks of ice; glaciers covered many parts of the earth a long time ago.

oxygen—the air that people, plants, and animals need to breathe

shallow—water that is not deep

To Learn More

AT THE LIBRARY

George, William T. *Box Turtle At Long Pond*. New York: Greenwillow Books, 1989.

Henderson, Kathy. *The Great Lakes*. Chicago: Childrens Press, 1989.

London, Jonathan. *Loon Lake*. San Francisco: Chronicle Books, 2002.

Wargin, Kathy-Jo. *The Edmund Fitzgerald: Song of the Bell*. Chelsea, Mich.: Sleeping Bear Press, 2003.

ON THE WEB

Learning more about lakes is as easy as 1, 2, 3.

1. Go to www.factsurfer.com

2. Enter "lakes" into search box.

3. Click the "Surf" button and you will see a list of related web sites.

With factsurfer.com, finding more information is just a click away.

Index